Puffins For Kids

Amazing Animal Books For Young Readers

By
Rachel Smith

Mendon Cottage Books
JD-Biz Corp Publishing

All Rights Reserved.

No part of this publication may be reproduced in any form or by any means, including scanning, photocopying, or otherwise without prior written permission from JD-Biz Corp

Copyright © 2015. All Images Licensed by Fotolia and 123RF.

Read More Amazing Animal Books

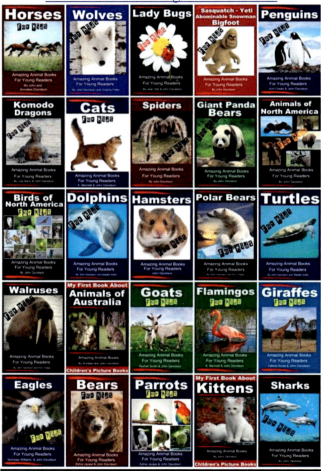

Purchase at Amazon.com

Table of Contents

Introduction 4

What is a puffin? 5

What kinds of puffins are there? 9

The history of puffins and humans 11

Atlantic puffin 14

Tufted puffin 19

Horned puffin 22

Conclusion 26

Author Bio 27

Publisher 28

Introduction

Puffins are adorable little creatures that sometimes remind people of penguins. Their coloring is a little similar to some sort of penguins, and they also live in cold regions, but that's where the similarities end.

They are big parts of the culture in places such as Iceland and the Faroe islands, and live in both the Atlantic Ocean area and the Pacific. Most people know very little about puffins, but they are fascinating creatures who have been the basis of survival for some and almost the symbol of their culture for others.

With their black and white bodies and their brilliantly colored beaks, puffins stand out among birds. They are not colorful like parrots or beautiful like swans, but the puffin has its own unique charms.

What is a puffin?

A puffin is a sort of Arctic bird. It falls into the category of auks within the genus Fratercula. They are a very specific type of bird, with only three (and possibly four) types within the genus. They are known as either auks or alcids, which are birds that live in cold areas.

A cluster of Atlantic puffins.

The puffin is a funny looking bird. Black and white is normal enough, but their brilliantly colored beaks might remind you of a clown's nose. However, their beaks are only colorful during mating season; after that, the colorful part falls off and they are left with smaller, duller colored beaks.

Fairly unique in their form of hunting, the puffin tends to life on coasts or overhangs over the sea. They live in huge numbers together, especially during breeding season. The puffin hunts like this: they fly high, with wingbeats of around 400 times per minute, over the ocean. Then, as soon as they spot a fish, they dive into the water, swimming as easily in the ocean as they fly in the air. The puffin swims in the same way it flies, flapping its wings as though it's in the air.

The puffin belongs to the genus Fratercula, which means something along the lines of 'little brother' in Latin. This is because their black and white coloring reminded the people who named them of monks, and since they are pretty small, it was only natural that the 'little' part should be added. The puffin also belongs to the subfamily Fraterculini, which includes all three types of puffin plus the rhinoceros auklet, which is most closely related to the puffin.

Puffins are believed to have come from the Pacific millions of years ago. One of the reasons for this belief is that the Pacific has two kinds of puffins in it, whereas the Atlantic only has one.

Puffins are usually silent. They can't alert anything to their coming, from the fish and such they want to catch to potential predators. However, when they are in their breeding colonies, the puffins make a very loud noise indeed. It sounds just like a chainsaw! It doesn't seem to fit their appearance, but that is the sound that adult puffins make.

As for breeding, puffins get together in huge numbers to do this. They will go into a colony on a coast or an island, and a nest will be built. In fact, so many of them show up, that there are a lot of places referred to as Puffin Island throughout their habitat.

Puffins prefer to breed in burrows, as it is much safer than doing it in the open and this is also where they raise their young. Puffins have been known not only to dig their own burrows, but also to take empty rabbit burrows.

Puffin chicks are often called pufflings. When the eggs are laid, one parent will use the brood-patch to keep the eggs warm. They take care of the pufflings, and eventually they're ready to fledge, which is done at night. The fledglings leave and go to sea for five years before returning to the colony to breed. In the winter, puffins tend to stay out at sea and avoid the land, such as their breeding colonies.

Iceland is considered to be a major puffin home, and it's no wonder; there are roughly ten million puffins on Iceland, which is over ten times the human population! The most puffin-populated place in the world is the Westmann Isles, which is a part of Iceland. About four million puffins live there.

Puffins are able to carry more than one fish in their mouths. Fish and zooplanktons are their source of food, though chicks only eat small fish. Puffins are able to carry more than one fish in their mouths because they have a special hinge to their beak, and it means they can move their beak around so that certain edges touch. Most other birds can only carry one fish at a time, or else they have to swallow it all and regurgitate (spit up) the fish for their young. Not the puffin, though; it can take long trips to find food because it can carry more food than other birds.

Long term relationships are very common with puffins when they breed. They are not the kind of animal that mates with as many as possible; instead, they are monogamous, meaning only a pair of mates, and no other puffins.

What kinds of puffins are there?

There three confirmed kinds, one very closely related bird, and at least one prehistoric kind.

A horned puffin.

First off, the prehistoric one: not a lot is known about it. It's called Dow's puffin, and it was named for a man who helped with paleontological expedition to find their fossils. Only a few skeletons and a lot of unattached bones have been found. It seems this puffin lived mostly in little islands off of California. One thing is for sure: they were pretty small birds.

The best known kind in the Western world is the Atlantic puffin. It is the only recognized puffin in the Atlantic. The theory is that all three of the main types of puffins started out as one in the Pacific, but some migrated towards the Atlantic; however, over time, the gap that they came through closed, and this puffin developed separately from the Pacific puffins. It is very common to Iceland and the Faroe Islands (a part of Denmark's territory).

Then there's the horned puffin. This one looks more like the Atlantic than the tufted puffin, but both the tufted and the horned puffin live in the Pacific. However, they have somewhat different ranges, and of course a physical difference as well.

Lastly, there is the rhinoceros auklet. It is a Pacific bird that does a lot of the things that the other puffins do, and it has been proposed that it be called the rhinoceros puffin instead, due to its very close relation. It is named the rhinoceros auklet because of the 'horn' on its beak, which looks similar to a rhinoceros (or rhino) horn. However, it is not a horn, but rather a part of its beak.

The puffin genus is fairly small, not like some genera that include a lot of species. Considering there are only three recognized puffins, that means that the puffin is not a very varied creature, even among its different species. Still, there are differences between each kind, and not just in appearance.

The history of puffins and humans

Puffins have long been important to humans. Not only are they adorable, but they have served a purpose to humans as well. The puffin is very popular as food, and was even more popular in the past. Now, it's a Faroese and Icelandic delicacy.

A tourist looking at puffins.

In Iceland, a very good delicacy is a puffin heart. They don't waste the puffin in Iceland because it is not a very good land for food, and much of it is uninhabitable anyway. The Icelanders have long relied on fish and seabirds for food, including the puffin. And it's no wonder, with the abundant numbers that live on Iceland.

Puffins have also been eaten by other groups. This includes a small island off of Ireland, where islanders could barely survive by hunting puffins. However, the island was abandoned in 1953, since life there was not really sustainable.

Here's a quick explanation of what Iceland and the Faroe Islands are. Iceland was an uninhabited island discovered by the Vikings, mostly the Norwegians. It was populated incredibly late in world history compared to most of the world, maybe a thousand years ago or so. It's a land that is so far north that during parts of the year, the Icelanders only get sunlight for a few hours a day. A good portion of Iceland is impossible to live in mainly due to volcanoes. Today, there are about 300,000 Icelanders living in Iceland, which is a very tiny population compared to the United States of America's 300 million or so.

Like Iceland, the Faroe Islands belonged to the Danes (the kingdom of Denmark) throughout much of history. Unlike Iceland, the Faroe Islands still belong to Denmark today. The Faroese, much like the Icelanders, got the short end of the stick from Denmark, isolated from other countries and forced to only trade with Denmark.

In both places, due to economies stifled by Denmark's policies, the puffin became an important source of food. They are the main two places in the world where it is legal to hunt puffins.

In the 19th and early 20th centuries, the puffin took a great hit to its numbers due to overhunting. Much like the passenger pigeon in America, which was hunted to extinction, the people who lived in areas that puffins lived in took advantage of new hunting techniques to catch as many as possible. Unlike the passenger pigeon, though, the puffin was given a chance to recover and is not endangered at all.

Puffins are hunted for their eggs, meat, and feathers.

Atlantic puffin

The Atlantic puffin is also known as the common puffin, because it's the most well-known in the English-speaking world. For a very long time, Europeans were not aware of the other kinds of puffins due to them living in the Pacific, an area that was not explored by Europeans for a very long time.

An Atlantic puffin sitting on a grassy cliff.

The Atlantic puffin lives mainly in the Scandinavian/Nordic area. This means, when they come to shore to breed, they mainly live in places like Greenland, Iceland, and Norway, and also in other North Atlantic islands. This means that their range can even extend to the British Isles and Maine in the United States.

The main difference between male and female is size, but even that is not a particularly large difference. It is hard to tell apart male and female Atlantic puffins. This is called a lack of sexual dimorphism; sexual dimorphism is when a female and a male look drastically different from each other in the same species, with every male and female.

An Atlantic puffin lives on the sea during autumn and winter, only coming during spring and summer to the shores. This is where they do their mating, in cliff colonies. That's not to say they won't nest anywhere else, but the Atlantic puffin much prefers an enclosed nest. They won't do an open nest like other birds. This is because they need to protect their flightless chick from predators. The Atlantic puffin lays only one egg, which is white.

There are a number of predators of the Atlantic puffin, not the least of which is humans. Besides us, however, there are also the skuas and the sea gulls. The skua will often attack puffins when they're bringing back food for their chick, forcing them to drop the food and leave it for the skua.

The Atlantic puffin is often called the 'Clown of the Sea' or the 'Sea Parrot.' This is because they are probably the most colorful sea creature in this area, kind of like the North's answer to the toucan or parrot.

Though their colorful beak parts come off, the average Icelander or Faroese Islander (among other places) tends to see them with their colorful beaks. Also, another reason that they are called those names is because of their silly-looking waddling walk.

When it is time for a chick to be fully-fledged (which means old enough to live on its own as a bird), which is usually about six weeks after being hatched, they will leave their nest and head down to the sea. It is important that they do this at night, as it is better cover from gulls and skuas, because there are few things these birds like better than a fresh-caught fledgling. The fledgling will then swim into the sea and stay there for a few years, until they themselves are old enough to mate.

There are three subspecies of Atlantic puffin: fratercula arctica arctica, fratercula arctica grabae, and fratercula arctica naumanni. However, the only real difference between them is in size, and some scientists argue that they should not be considered subspecies at all. Basically, with these birds, the farther North you go, the bigger the bird will be, and this is why there are three subspecies.

The interesting thing about the Atlantic puffin is its appearance. The eye looks almost triangular (shaped like a triangle) because of the gray patch around it. And the beak is slate gray near the back, and orange near the front; from the top, it looks narrow, and from the side, broad and also triangular. When the outer beak falls off, it's not nearly so colorful. This is called molting, and they lose other facial features too, such as the gray around their eyes. They lose most of what makes them stand out when they go back to sea.

When the Atlantic puffins go to sea, they live in a different way than on land. Not a lot is known about their life at sea, because it's really hard to find them. One reason for this is that they live alone when they're at sea. Rather than being a flock, each individual bird could be miles from the next one. It's incredibly difficult to pick out a human in the ocean; it's even harder to pick out an individual puffin.

But how do they live if they have nowhere to land? Easy answer: they float. The Atlantic puffin spends its time at sea mostly floating on the surface of the water and using its webbed feet to push itself along. They will also dive to get food when they are out in the ocean.

What's interesting about this bird is that, unlike land birds, which lose their primary feathers during molting one wing at a time so they can still sort of fly, the puffin loses all its primary feathers at once. It cannot fly at all for a month or two while it's out at sea. So, it swims instead.

When it does fly, the puffin tends to patter along the surface of the water, wings flapping, until it can take off. Then, when landing in the water, it tends to awkwardly crash into it.

The Atlantic puffin eats mostly small fish, though it has been known to eat crustaceans (like little crabs, for example) and shrimp as well, among other things. However, its main food is definitely small fish. It can eat fish up eighteen centimeters long, though it tends to go for shorter fish.

This kind of puffin deals with the excess salt in its food and the water it consumes by its strong kidneys and its salt secreting glands.

Tufted puffin

The tufted puffin is also known as the crested puffin.

A tufted puffin in an aquarium.

They are around 35 centimeters long. The tufted puffin doesn't have as much white on it as the Atlantic puffin, and instead only has a small patch of white. Its beak is a bit different too; it's a bright red, with some orange and sometimes green. It's named for the long tufts on the top of its head.

When it comes time for molting, or the non-mating season, they lose their bright colors, not just their beak, but also their white patch, leg colors, and their tufts.

A funny thing about this type of puffin is that their juveniles (not quite grown up puffins) are a brownish color, with a whitish belly. This means they look different from the blackish-bluish molted puffins, and for a while, the juveniles were named as a different genus, the Latham's saddle-billed auk. This mistake was fixed, though.

Tufted puffins nest in places like Alaska, Kamchatka (part of Russia across from Alaska), the Aleutian Islands, British Columbia, and so on. It tends towards the East Pacific, however, leaving room for the other puffin that lives in the Pacific.

They like cliffs for their nesting, mostly digging holes in loose dirt for their nests, but sometimes using crevices too. They like areas that are secluded, hard to reach for predators, easy to take flight from, and have plenty of fish in the waters. This means they usually nest on isolated islands.

They eat many similar things to the Atlantic puffin, though they have also been known to eat squid.

Tufted puffins are hunted by a number of creatures, mostly birds. This includes the snowy owl, the bald eagle, and the peregrine falcon, on top of predators such as the Arctic fox, which seems to really prefer puffins to other birds.

This type of puffin was long caught by the Aleut and Ainu peoples, and their skins were used for parkas. The tufts were also used for decorations. However, nowadays, the hunting of the tufted puffin is mostly banned or discouraged.

Horned puffin

The horned puffin is so named because of a black sort of fleshy horn above its eye. It looks a lot more like the Atlantic puffin than the tufted puffin does.

A horned puffin swimming.

Its beak is a bit different from the other two's, though. It has red at the tip, and the main part is yellow. The colors come off during feeding season, like with the other puffins.

Like the other two, this type of puffin eats small fish, and feeds its chick with them.

It also goes out to sea for many months, as plain-looking as its fellow puffins. However, it is still distinguishable from the tufted puffin.

It lives in the Pacific, nesting on rocky islands; these include the shorelines of Alaska, British Columbia, and Siberia. They like to nest in rocky burrows, crevices, or just among rocks.

The big danger to these birds, though it is not endangered, consists of rats. Many places that they used to nest safely on are overrun with rats, which were unwittingly introduced by humans. The rats eat their eggs and chicks.

Rhinoceros auklet

The rhinoceros auklet is considered a puffin by some, sometimes called the unicorn puffin or the horn-billed puffin. However, it is not generally recognized by the community of zoologists. That said, it is more closely related to the tufted puffin than the other puffins are.

A rhinoceros auklet, near Japan.

The rhino auklet is so named for its horn. Like the puffins, it loses the horn when it's not mating season anymore. Also like the puffins, it nests in colonies.

Rhino auklets also live in the North Pacific, from the Aleutian Islands to California on the North America side, to North Korea and parts of Japan in the Asian waters.

They like deep burrows, anywhere from one meter to five meters deep. Every night, long after incubating the egg together and hatching the chick, the baby is fed a bunch of fish.

They also go inshore, which is not typical of puffins.

The rhino auklet is also the only living member of its genus.

Conclusion

Puffins are interesting, cute little creatures. As the symbol of British Columbia, and other places, it's amazing how much the puffin has influenced the cultures of the world.

From the Ainu and Aleuts who used them for both food and parkas, to the Icelanders and Faroese who hunted them through sky fishing, the puffin made many places habitable for new peoples.

Hopefully, they will continue to be a great feature of cultures in the North.

Author Bio

Rachel Smith is a young author who enjoys animals. Once, she had a rabbit which was very nervous, and chewed through her leash and tried to escape. She's also had several pet mice, which were the funniest little animals to watch. She lives in Ohio with her family and writes in her spare time.

Publisher

JD-Biz Corp

P O Box 374

Mendon, Utah 84325

http://www.jd-biz.com/

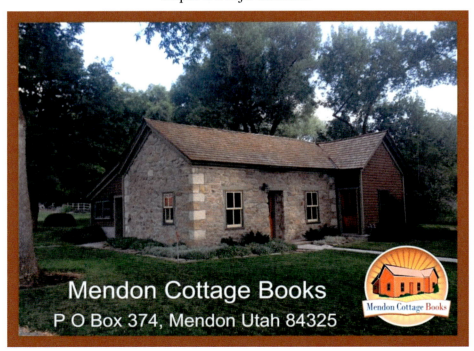

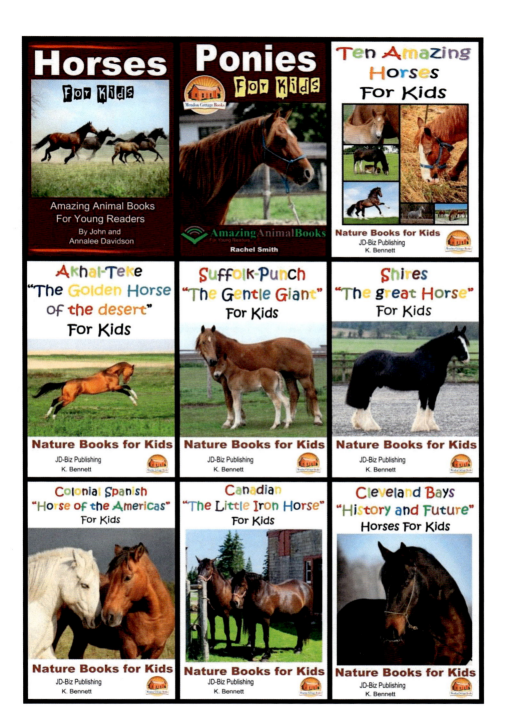

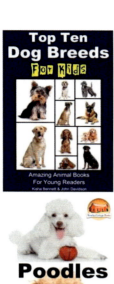

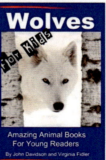

Puffins

Puffins Page 33

Manufactured by Amazon.ca
Bolton, ON